GOD IS WITH YOU ALL THE TIME

CHERYL PICKETT

Published by Brighter Day Publishing
USA

Copyright © 2021

ISBN: 978-0-9841855-4-2

Contact: For more information please visit:
www.cherylpickett.com

Printed in the United States of America

Scripture quotations are from the ESV® Bible (The Holy Bible,
English Standard Version®), Copyright © 2001 by Crossway,
a publishing ministry of Good News Publishers. Used by
permission. All rights reserved.

If you travel near or far,

When you're riding in a car,

God is everywhere
you are.

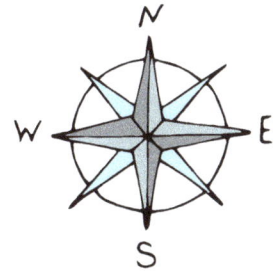

If you fly way, way up high,

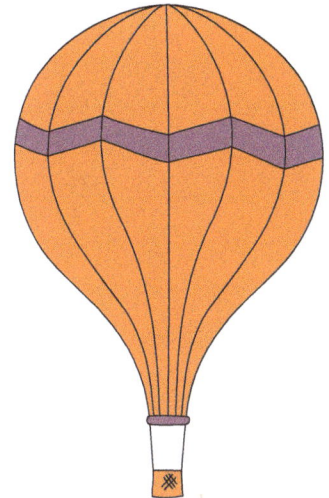

or ride a balloon

into the sky,

God will never

say goodbye.

If you go down deep below,

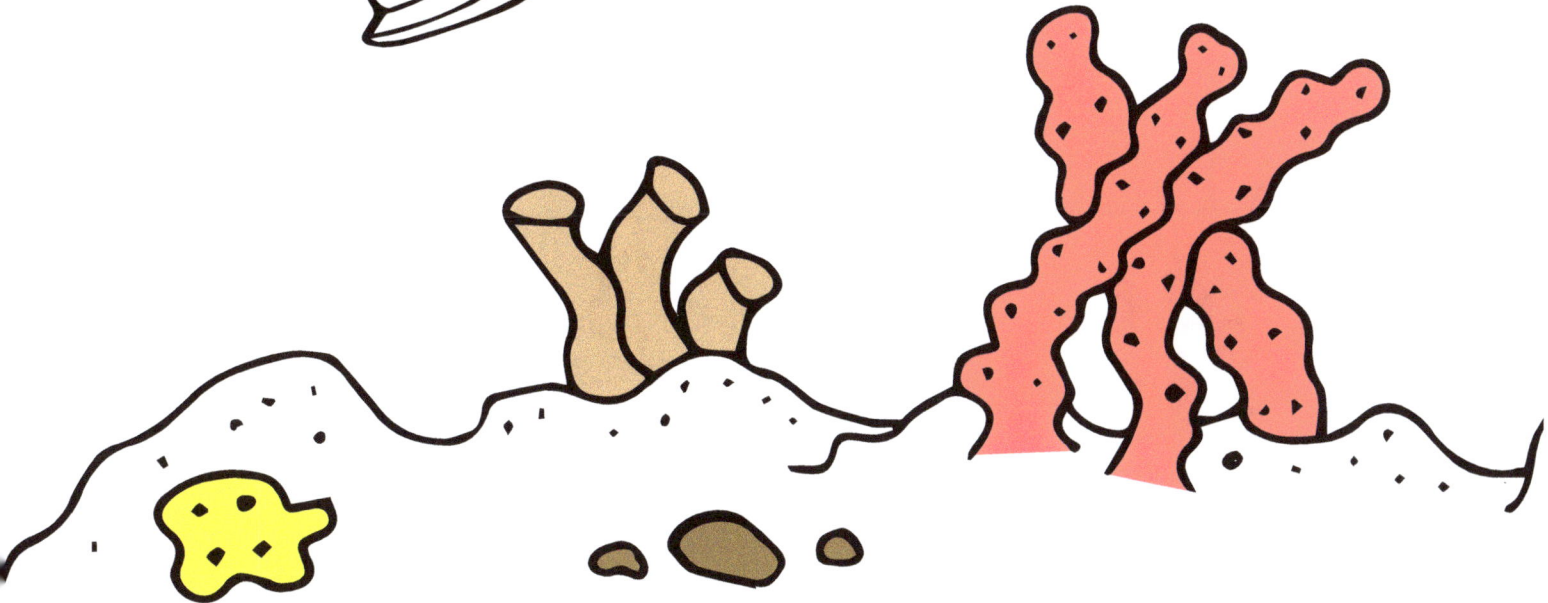

deep under the sea

where the big fish grow,

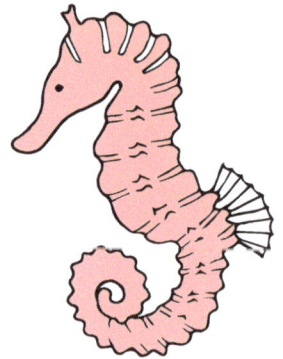

God is everywhere

you'll go.

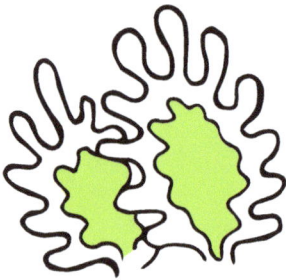

If it's time to
play outside,

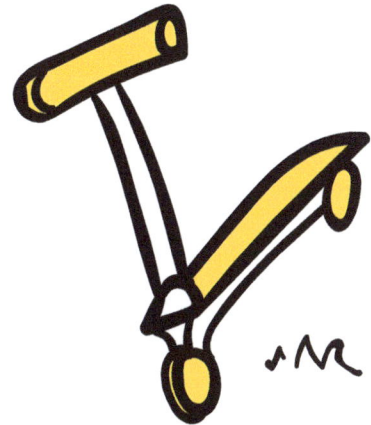

swing on

the swing,

slide down the slide,

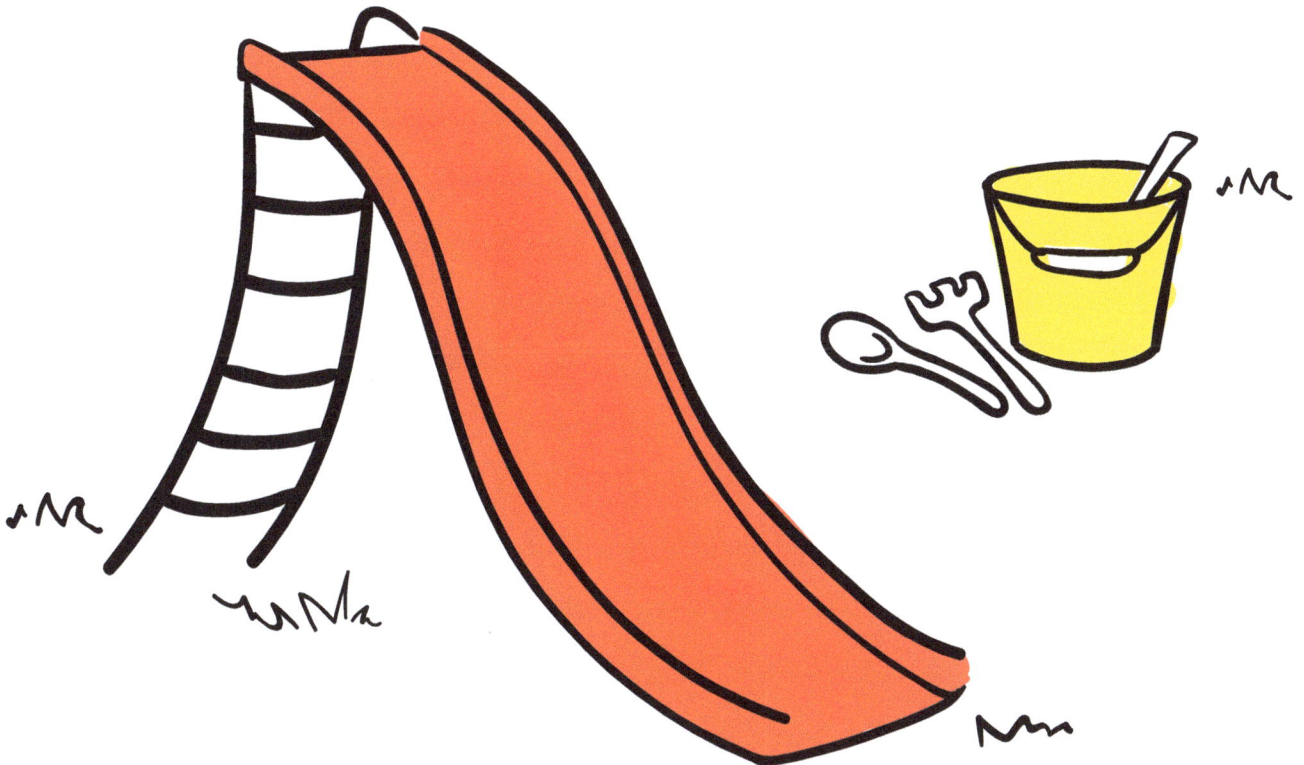

God is always

by your side.

No matter where
you like to play,

In the sand,

or in the spray,

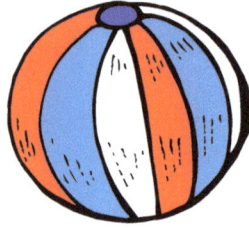
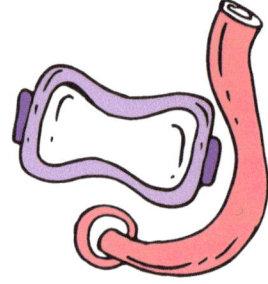

God is never

far away.

If the clock says

now it's night,

If it's time to turn

out the lights,

God is there,

happy dreams,

sleep tight.

If it's time to

ride the bus,

time to read,

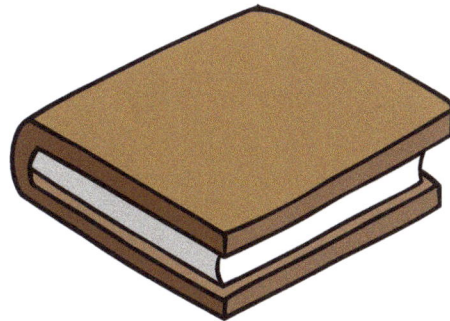

or learn minus
and plus,

2+2=4

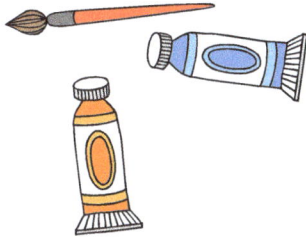
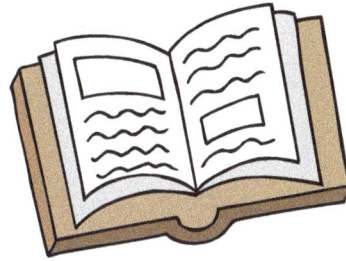

God is with you,

no need to fuss.

$2+2=4$

ABC

When the sky turns dark and
swirly,

When the storm clouds
are in a hurry,

God is with you,

no need to worry.

When you're feeling

sad or blue,

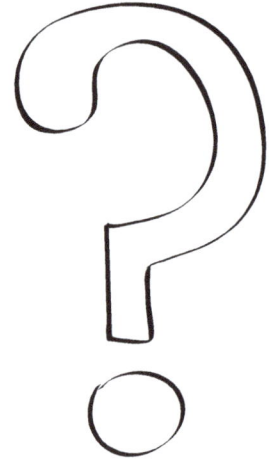

When you don't
know what you'll do,

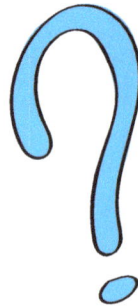

God is always

there for you.

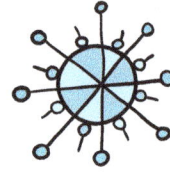

He sends the white
and sparkling snow,

He sends the rain

so flowers grow,

He made the sun and moon
that shine,

GOD IS WITH YOU ALL THE TIME.

GOD IS WITH US!
THE BIBLE TELLS US SO!

Psalm 100:5

3 Know that the LORD, he is God!
It is he who made us, and we are his;
we are his people, and the sheep of his pasture.

4 Enter his gates with thanksgiving,
and his courts with praise!
Give thanks to him; bless his name!

5 For the LORD is good;
his steadfast love endures forever,
and his faithfulness to all generations.